DESIGN YOUR TOMORROW, TODAY

YOUR PATH TO A BLISSFUL

RETIREMENT

I0407639

VERONICA SYLVESTER

Table of contents

INTRODUCTION

Take a deep breath and close your eyes. Imagine yourself on a peaceful beach, with golden sands reaching out in front of you and a soft breeze rustling through the pages of your favorite book. The warm sun warms you as you sip a nice drink. This is just one chapter in your retirement story, a story that combines the serenity of the beach with the warmth of a fireside afternoon. We'll help you create a retirement plan that allows you to enjoy both beach vacations and cozy nights by the fire, all while ensuring financial security and unlimited adventures.

☐ **What is Retirement**

Retirement is the stage of life in which a person leaves the employment voluntarily, generally after reaching a certain age or meeting specified criteria set by their employer or government. Individuals in retirement stop working for a regular paycheck and often rely on savings, pensions, social security, or other retirement income sources to cover their living expenditures. After years of working, this is a time for rest, relaxation, and pursuing personal hobbies. To maintain financial security throughout this time, retirement planning is essential.

☐ Why Retirement Planning Matters

Retirement planning matters for several important reasons:

Financial Security

Retirement planning ensures that you have the financial means to support yourself during your retirement years. It helps you avoid running out of money when you no longer have a regular income from work.

Maintaining Lifestyle

It allows you to maintain your desired lifestyle in retirement. Without proper planning, you might have to significantly downgrade your standard of living after retiring.

Independence

Adequate retirement planning provides you with financial independence. You won't have to rely solely on family members or government assistance to meet your basic needs.

Healthcare Costs

As you age, healthcare expenses tend to increase. Retirement planning helps cover medical costs and long-term care, reducing the financial burden on you and your loved ones.

Peace of Mind

Knowing that you have a well-thought-out retirement plan in place can bring peace of mind. You'll have a clearer picture of your financial future and can enjoy retirement without constant worry.

Legacy Planning

Retirement planning allows you to leave a financial legacy for your loved ones or support charitable causes you care about.

Adaptation

Life is unpredictable, and unexpected expenses or changes in circumstances can occur. Retirement planning provides flexibility to adapt to these changes.

Tax Efficiency

Proper planning can help you minimize tax liabilities in retirement, allowing you to keep more of your savings.

Inflation Protection

Planning for retirement involves strategies to protect your savings from the eroding effects of inflation, ensuring your purchasing power remains intact.

Longevity

People are living longer, which means retirement could last several decades. Adequate planning ensures your savings can sustain you throughout your entire retirement.

It is worthy to note that retirement planning is essential to achieve financial security, maintain your desired lifestyle, and enjoy a worry-free retirement. It's an investment in your future well-being and peace of mind.

Chapter 1

Understanding retirement

☐ Defining Your Retirement Goals

Setting goals for retirement is essential to creating a safe and satisfying retirement. Start by thinking about:

Financial Objectives

Establish your required income, sources of retirement income (savings, pensions, Social

Security), and growth-oriented investment strategies.

Determine where you'll live, how you'll spend your time, and any travel or activities you'd like to take up in your lifestyle goals.

Healthcare Objectives

Budget for medical costs, such as insurance and anticipated long-term care requirements. Retirement home fee is you or a family member will be staying in one.

Social Objectives

Think about your social network, how you'll keep in touch with people, and how you'll stay active in your neighborhood.

Consider your legacy goals, such as how you want to support loved ones or worthy charities.

Timeline

Establish a retirement age and checkpoints for completing your objectives. Be prepared to review and modify your objectives as the situation evolves. It is necessary to seek the assistance of a financial advisor.

☐ Retirement Age and Options

The retirement age and possibilities might change depending on the nation and the individual. The average retirement age is 65 to 67 years old in many nations, but it's important to confirm what age applies to your nation's social security system or pension plan.

Regarding retirement choices, they can be:

Social Security

In the United States and many other nations, you can apply for Social Security benefits at a variety of ages, with full payments available at your full retirement age (usually 65–67) and reduced benefits if you start sooner (as early as 62).

Pensions

Some firms give regular payments upon retirement through pension schemes.

Personal retirement assets, such as those held in 401(k)s or IRA accounts, may be used to supplement income in retirement.

Annuities

These financial instruments can offer a consistent flow of income of earnings in return for a one-time payment.

Part-Time Employment

To supplement their retirement income, many people decide to work part-time. Do not do any strenuous Job, you can work as a yoga/instructor if you're into sports, or grow your own garden.

Investments

The money you receive from stocks, bonds, or real estate might go toward funding your retirement. Therefore it is important to invest while working and have a multiple stream of passive income.

Downsizing

You can free up money for retirement by selling your larger property and moving into a smaller, more inexpensive one. You can modify to make more homey and comfortable.

To find the best retirement alternatives for your particular situation, it's critical to start planning for retirement early, think about your financial goals, and speak with a financial counselor.

☐ Retirement Lifestyle Planning

Retirement lifestyle planning entails examining your financial needs and retirement goals. Consider your preferred lifestyle, healthcare costs, and anticipated retirement age. To ensure a pleasant retirement, it is critical to save and invest intelligently, maybe with the assistance of a financial counselor.

Chapter 2

Financial Foundations

☐ Assessing Your Financial Situation/Creating Your Retirement Budget

Determine your sources of retirement income, such as pensions, social security, savings, and any other investments. Calculate your retirement income.

Needs

Make a list of your anticipated retirement costs, including mandatory needs like housing, healthcare, and groceries as well as optional spending.

Budget

Create a thorough budget to balance your income and expenses. Make sure your spending plan include room for emergencies and unforeseen costs.

Debt

Evaluate and take care of any unpaid loans or mortgages. More of your retirement income may be available if you reduce or pay off your debt. Also avoid unnecessary debts if you can, as it can affect your retirement plan greatly.

Review your Portfolio of Investments

Think about investing in a variety of assets that fit your risk appetite and financial objectives. Many retirees place a high priority on maintaining income and investments.

Create an Emergency Fund

Keep an emergency fund on hand to pay for unforeseen costs. Typically, it is advised to have three to six months' worth of living expenses saved up.

Healthcare

Be aware of your insurance options, including Medicare and any supplemental plans. Think about possible long-term care requirements. Also make provisions for alternative healthcare resources.

Estate Planning

To make sure your assets are dispersed in accordance with your preferences, review and amend your will, beneficiary designations, and estate plans. Ensure everything is in place and according to your preference ofcourse.

Tax Planning

Recognize how your investments and sources of retirement income will affect your taxes. You can increase your income by using techniques like tax-efficient withdrawals.

Inflation

Take this into account while making your financial plans. Your purchasing power will be impacted if prices increase over time so do well to seal any loops.

Determine when to begin applying for Social Security benefits. Depending on your unique situation, delaying could result in higher monthly payments.

Monitor and modify your financial strategy as necessary as conditions change, such as market swings, fluctuations in the market, health status or family needs.

Transition into Retirement

To ensure your savings and investments last during retirement, plan how you'll access them and ensure you follow that plan so things don't get mixed up.

Chapter 3

Retirement accounts

☐ 401(k)s and IRAs

Both IRAs and 401(k)s are retirement savings accounts that provide tax benefits to encourage and enable people to save for retirement:

401(k)s

Employer-sponsored: 401(k)s are frequently provided by businesses, and employees may make pre-tax contributions to the accounts.

Tax benefits: Contributions are tax-deferred, so you won't have to pay taxes on them until you take them out in retirement.

Employer matching: A few firms will match a portion of your retirement savings, effectively giving you free money.

Limitations on contributions: There are annual restrictions on the amount you can put into a 401(k)s.

Individual Retirement Accounts (IRAs)

Individual: IRAs are not opened by employers; rather, individuals do themselves.

Tax benefits: Traditional and Roth IRAs are the two main varieties. Contributions to traditional IRAs are tax deductible, while

RothRetirement withdrawals from IRAs are tax-free.

More investment alternatives: Compared to 401(k)s, where your options are often constrained to what your company offers, IRAs frequently offer more investment options.

Contribution ceilings: Annual contribution ceilings for IRAs exist as well, albeit they are often lower than 401(k) ceilings.

Depending on your employment status, income level, and retirement objectives, you should decide between a 401(k) and an IRA. To optimize their retirement funds, many choose both. While Roth IRAs offer tax-free withdrawals in retirement but no immediate tax break, traditional 401(k)s and IRAs offer immediate tax benefits. A financial advisor must be consulted in order to develop a retirement savings plan that is appropriate for you, please endeavor to consult one.

☐ Pension Plans

Retirement income payments are regularly made to retirees through financial arrangements called pension plans. Pension plans come in a variety of forms, including:

Employers

Plans with defined benefits guarantee a predetermined benefit amount depending on variables including pay and years of service. These plans are often managed and funded by employers.

Contribution Plans

Examples of defined contribution plans are 401(k)s and IRAs. These programs let employees and occasionally employers to make financial contributions to particular accounts that are then invested. The contributions and investment returns determine the final payout.

Government Pensions

Employees in the public sector frequently have access to pension programs like Social Security in the US or the Canada Pension Plan in Canada.

Annuities

Annuities are insurance policies that offer recurring payouts, and some retirees acquire them.in return for a one-time payment.

Personal Savings

To finance their retirement, many retirees rely on personal savings, including individual investments, savings accounts, or other assets.

To secure financial security during your retirement years, it is crucial to plan for retirement and weigh your possibilities. Making decisions about pension plans and retirement funds with knowledge might be facilitated by consulting a financial advisor.

☐ Social Security Benefits

In many nations, including the United States, Social Security benefits for retirees constitute a government-provided financial safety net. Although specifics vary by country, here is some general information concerning Social Security payouts for retirees in the United States:

Eligibility

To be eligible for Social Security retirement benefits in the United States, you must have worked and paid Social Security taxes for a specified number of years. The exact amount of credits needed is determined by your birth year.

Full Retirement Age (FRA)

The age at which you can receive full Social Security retirement benefits is known as your FRA. It used to be 65, but for individuals born in 1960 or later, it has steadily grown to 67. You can still opt to begin receiving benefits as early as age 62, but they will be lowered if you do so before your FRA.

The amount of your monthly Social Security retirement payment is determined by your lifetime earnings and the age you begin collecting benefits. Benefits delayed beyond your FRA may result in higher monthly payments.

Spousal Benefits

If you are married, you may be entitled to spousal benefits based on your spouse's earnings history. Spousal benefits might be up to 50% of the benefit amount of your spouse.

Survivor payments

Social Security pays survivor payments to widows, widowers, and dependents of dead workers who are qualified.

Taxation

A part of your Social Security benefits may be subject to federal income tax depending on your overall income.

It is essential to get particular information regarding retirement benefits, such as qualifying criteria, benefit calculations, and the application process, from your country's Social Security administration or equivalent agency. Consider consulting a financial expert to assist you in making informed decisions about when to claim

your Social stability payments in order to

enhance your financial stability throughout

retirement.

Chapter 4

Investment strategies

□ Diversification and Risk

Management

Diversification of Assets

Retirees should diversify their investments

among asset types such as stocks, bonds, and

real estate. This lessens the impact of a single area's bad performance.

Risk Tolerance

Recognize your risk tolerance. You may prefer a more cautious portfolio as a retiree to protect your funds. Consider how much risk you are willing to accept.

Multiple Income Streams

Concentrate on developing a consistent income stream. Dividend-paying stocks and bonds can provide consistent income to cover living expenses. It is also advisable to have multiple streams of income, preferably passive incomes.

Maintaining an emergency fund in a low-risk, liquid account is a good idea. This can help you pay unforeseen expenses and avoid having to sell investments during a downturn.

Long-Term View

Retirement can last decades. Don't get too caught up in short-term market volatility. Maintain a long-term perspective and avoid impulsive decision.

Work with Financial Advisors

Working with financial experts can help you manage your finances and reach your financial objectives. They can advise on investing, retirement planning, tax strategy, and other topics. Consider an advisor's qualifications, pricing, and communication style when selecting one to ensure a suitable fit for your needs.

Chapter 5

Healthcare and insurance

☐ Medicare and Medicaid

While Medicaid is intended to provide healthcare coverage to low-income individuals and families, encompassing a wider range of age groups and vulnerable populations, Medicare primarily serves older persons and some people with disabilities. Different groups of the American population can receive healthcare thanks in large part to these initiatives.

Both Medicare and Medicaid are government health insurance programs in the US, however they cater to distinct demographics and have different goals

Medicare

Medicare is a government health insurance program that is primarily intended for people over 65. Some younger people with disabilities are also covered.

- Part A (Hospital Insurance)

- Part B (Medical Insurance)

- Part C (Medicare Advantage)

- Part D (Drug Prescription Coverage)

  make up its four components.

The care provided in skilled nursing facilities, hospices, and to some extent in some homes is included in Part A.

Doctor's services, outpatient treatment, preventative services, and medical supplies are all covered in Part B.

Beneficiaries may get their Medicare benefits through private insurance plans under Part C. Prescription drugs are covered by Part D.

Medicaid

Medicaid is a cooperative state-federal program that offers providing low-income individuals and families with access to healthcare.

States have the freedom to choose how to design their own Medicaid requirements, thus eligibility and benefits may differ from one state to the next.

Numerous medical services are covered by Medicaid, including doctor visits, hospital stays, prescription medications, and long-term care.

It assists low-income persons as well as several vulnerable groups, including pregnant women, children, and people with impairments.

☐ Long-term Care Insurance

In order to cover the costs of services and support for those who require assistance with everyday tasks due to aging, illness, or disability, long-term care insurance was created. For elders, it's important to keep in mind the following:

Coverage: Services including nursing facility care, assisted living, in-home care, and adult day care are frequently covered by long-term care insurance.

Premiums: Premiums have a tendency to becoming more expensive as people age. Budget for these expenses and pick an insurance plan that works with your budget.

Seniors may need to meet specific health requirements in order to be eligible for coverage, so it's better to buy a policy when you're still in reasonably good health.

Benefit Period: The duration of care coverage varies amongst policies. Some possess a set while others provide coverage for a lifetime.

The waiting period before benefits start is known as the elimination period. You'll get coverage faster if the elimination period is shorter, but your premiums can go up.

Consider insurance with inflation protection to make sure that benefits keep up with escalating healthcare costs.

There are both conventional long-term care policies and hybrid policies, which combine long-term care with an annuity or a life insurance policy. Find out which choice best meets your needs.

Consult a Financial Advisor: To make an informed choice given the complexity of these products, it is recommended that you speak with a financial advisor who focuses on retirement planning.

Specific State Regulations: State laws governing long-term care insurance can differ, so it's important toknow the local regulations that apply.

Review Your coverage Periodically: As you become older and your circumstances change, make sure your insurance coverage still satisfies your needs.

Long-term care insurance can provide seniors piece of mind by helping them pay for care, but it's important to do your homework and pick the best plan for your particular scenario.

☐ Health Savings Accounts (HSAs)

HSAs (Health Savings Accounts) are primarily made for those with high-deductible health insurance plans who want to set aside money for eligible medical costs. For elders, there are a few things to keep in mind:

Eligibility

Seniors 65 and over who are not enrolled in Medicare Part A, Part B, or any other Medicare plan are still eligible to have an HSA. They can no longer make contributions to an HSA after they are enrolled in Medicare.

Rollover

Seniors can use their current HSA funds for eligible medical costs, including as prescription medicines, Medicare premiums, deductibles, and copayments. HSAs can be an excellent resource for paying for these costs.

After age 65, seniors may withdraw money from their HSAs without being subject to a 20% penalty; however, income tax will still be due. The withdrawals are treated the same as withdrawals from regular IRAs.

Savings for the Future

Seniors who keep their HSA in good standing can use it as a tax-advantaged method of saving for conceivable future medical bills, including long-term care costs.

Medicare Coordination

It's critical to comprehend how HSAs work with Medicare and supplemental insurance programs. Seniors who need assistance navigating the complexity might speak with a financial counselor or tax expert.

Overall, HSAs for seniors can be advantageous, but when they become eligible for Medicare, the rules and implications change, so it's important to plan appropriately.

Chapter 6

Estate Planning

☐ Wills and Trusts

Seniors can guarantee that their assets are managed and dispersed in accordance with their preferences by using wills and trusts, which are crucial legal tools. Here is a quick summary:

Wills

A will is a formal document that lays out the distribution of a person's possessions and assets following their passing.

Seniors ought to think about writing or revising their wills to include specific instructions for beneficiaries, guardians for small children (if appropriate), and an executor to carry out their desires.

To make sure the will is legally solid and complies with state regulations, it is advisable to speak with an attorney with experience in estate planning.

Healthcare Power of Attorney and Living Will

A living will, also known as an advance healthcare directive, is a document that defines a person's wishes for medical care in the event that they become incapable of speaking.

A person can designate a healthcare proxy to make medical decisions on their behalf.

Trusts

Trusts are flexible mechanisms that can assist elders in managing and allocating assets both throughout their lifetime and after they pass away.

Assets can avoid probate with the use of revocable living trusts, potentially saving time and money.

Assets may be protected from some taxes and creditors with the aid of irrevocable trusts.

To decide which kind of trust is best for your particular case, speak with an attorney.

Estate Management

Organizing assets, taking tax implications into account, and ensuring a seamless wealth transfer to heirs are all part of estate planning. Seniors should frequently evaluate and revise their estate plans, particularly if their personal or family circumstances change.

Legal Support

Seniors are strongly advised to speak with a lawyer who specializes in these. Legal documents should be drafted or updated using elder law and estate planning.

Legal experts can assist in modifying the documents to satisfy particular demands and guarantee adherence to state legislation.

Designations of Beneficiaries

The beneficiary designations on your retirement accounts, life insurance policies, and other financial assets should be current and consistent with your entire estate plan.

Keep in mind that estate planning is a complicated topic, and the specifics can change depending on a person's situation and the rules of their state. To build a thorough and legally solid strategy for elders, professional advice is required.

☐ Power of Attorney

A power of attorney is a legal document that grants one person **(the "principal")** the ability to make decisions and execute actions on their behalf to another person **(the "agent" or "attorney-in-fact")**. Depending on the sort of power of attorney, this can encompass financial, legal, or healthcare choices. It's a vital legal tool that's frequently used for estate planning and making sure someone's affairs are managed if they become disabled. Specific rules governing powers of attorney differ by jurisdiction, thus it is critical to speak with an attorney before drafting one.

☐ Inheritance and Tax considerations

Depending on your region and unique circumstances, inheritance and tax issues can differ dramatically. In general, there could be tax repercussions when someone inherits money or property. Here are some important things to think about:

Estate Tax

Some countries or states impose taxes on the estate of the deceased person before assets are distributed to heirs. The threshold and rates can vary.

Inheritance Tax

In certain places, heirs may be subject to an inheritance tax on the assets they receive. The tax rate and exemptions differ by jurisdiction.

Gift Tax

If someone gives you a significant gift, it could be subject to gift tax. However, there are often exemptions and limits in place.

Capital Gains Tax

If you inherit assets like stocks or real estate and later sell them, you may be liable for capital gains tax based on the increase in value from the time of inheritance.

Step-Up in Basis

In some regions, the cost basis of inherited assets is **"stepped up"** to the market value at the time of the original owner's death. This can reduce capital gains tax when you sell the assets.

Estate Planning

Proper estate planning can help minimize tax liabilities through trusts, gifting strategies, and other mechanisms.

Probate

The process of distributing assets through probate can also have legal and administrative costs, which should be considered.

Local Regulations

Tax laws and regulations are subject to change and can vary widely, so it's important to consult with a tax professional or attorney familiar with your jurisdiction.

Exemptions and Deductions

Look into any available exemptions, deductions, or credits that can help reduce the tax burden.

It's crucial to consult with a qualified tax advisor or attorney who can provide personalized guidance based on your specific situation and location, as the details can be complex and subject to change.

Chapter 7

Lifestyle Choices

☐ Downsizing and Housing Options

Independent Living Communities

Independent living communities are apartment-style homes intended for elderly who are still active. They lessen the burdens of homeownership while providing a range of facilities and activities.

Facilities for assisted living

These allow some independence while helping with everyday duties like food, medication, and personal care.

Continuing Care Retirement Communities (CCRCs)

CCRCs enable seniors to age in place by providing a range of care levels, from independent living to skilled nursing.

Apartments for seniors

These are frequently more compact, low-maintenance apartments.

Aging in Place

To make their current residences more pleasant and accessible as they age, you can make modifications.

Shared Housing

To cut costs and fight isolation, seniors can live in a house or apartment with others.

ADUs (accessory dwelling units)

These are scaled-down,self-contained units that are added to an existing building to provide seniors or carers with separate living space.

☐ Travel and Hobbies

Hobbies

Grow a Garden

Start a garden in your backyard or participate in a neighborhood community garden. It can be relaxing and pleasant to grow flowers, veggies, or herbs.

Creative Activities

Take up photography, painting, or drawing. To develop your abilities, go to workshops or classes.

Musical Instruments

Retirement is a perfect time to start learning an instrument if you've always wanted to. Think about the piano, the guitar, or even a novel instrument like the ukulele.

Sports and Fitness

Take up an activity you like, like swimming, tennis, or golf, badminton or join a fitness club. A healthy retirement depends on maintaining an active lifestyle.

Crafting

Look into hobbies like pottery, woodworking, or knitting. These are both creative and unwinding.

Reading and Writing

Get lost in a book.

Whether it's journaling, short tales, or memoirs, make a list of writing projects you've always wanted to take on or give a try. Join a book club too.

Travel

Start by getting to know your neighborhood by visiting any museums, parks, or historical locations you may have missed.

Interstate travel

Visit family and friends across the nation, take road trips to various states, or explore national parks.

Global Adventures

If you have the funds and the desire, think about going abroad. Discover various locations, foods, and cultures.

Live the Cruise

Consider living the cruise or RV life to comfortably visit several different locations. For many people, it's a common retirement option.

Volunteering

While traveling is a fulfilling way to travel and work at the same time. You can travel and help local communities at the same time.

Participate in Travel Clubs

Clubs or organizations geared for retirees. They frequently plan group outings and provide fellowship.

Consider your interests, health, and finances while planning your retirement hobbies and vacations. Create a wish list, establish goals, and give top priority to activities that will make you happy and fulfilled.

☐ Staying Active and Healthy

Regular Workouts

As advised by the World Health Organization (WHO), aim for at least 150 minutes of moderate-intensity aerobic activity or 75 minutes of vigorous-intensity aerobic activity per week.

Walking, swimming, cycling, and even gardening are examples of activities.

To maintain muscle mass and bone density, perform strength training exercises at least twice per week.

Social Interaction

Maintain relationships with friends and family to keep your emotional health.

Join clubs, local organizations, or volunteer groups to make new friends and maintain your social life.

Develop Hobbies

Take part in your passions, whether they are cooking, painting, playing an instrument, or any other pastime.

Hobbies offer mental challenge and a sense of direction.

Healthy Eating

Maintain a diet full of fresh produce, whole grains, lean meats, and other healthy foods. Take in plenty of water to stay hydrated. Limit your intake of processed meals, too much sugar, and salt.

Regular Medical Exams

Make appointments with your healthcare practitioner on a regular basis to monitor your health and address any issues. Follow the age-appropriate immunization and screening schedule.

Mental Wellness

Put your mental health first by practicing stress management techniques like yoga, meditation, or mindfulness.

If you experience sadness, anxiety, or other mental health problems, get professional assistance.

Stay Up to Date

Keep up with retirement planning and health-related news.

Know any potential health concerns associated with aging and how to manage or prevent them.

Plan your finances

To alleviate stress and protect your health in retirement, make sure you have enough money.

Hire a financial advisor to help you manage your retirement funds and travel and exploration, investing. Take advantage of your retirement to travel and discover new things.

A fantastic approach to keep active and involved is to travel.

Sleep

Give quality sleep a high priority for your overall health and energy levels.

Sleep for 7-9 hours every night.

Keep in mind that maintaining a healthy lifestyle in retirement is a lifetime commitment. Make lifestyle decisions based on your preferences and capabilities, and seek out individualized counsel and direction from healthcare professionals. Take full advantage of this new stage of life!

Chapter 8

Social and emotional well-being

☐ Building a Supportive Network

For general well-being as a senior or retiree, developing a supportive network is crucial. Here are some actions to think about:

Maintain Connection with Loved Ones: Maintain connections with your friends, family, and past coworkers. Loneliness can be fought off by regular social encounters.

Join Groups or Clubs: Look for clubs or organizations in your area that share your interests. It might result in new friendships.

Volunteer: Make a time and talent donation to a cause that matters to you. A nice approach to make new friends and stay active in your community is by volunteering.

Online Communities: Look into social networks and forums with a focus on seniors or your particular hobbies. They may offer a feeling of comfort and kinship.

Attend workshops and classes: Continuing education is a fantastic way to connect with people who share your interests.. Search online or at nearby community centers for workshops or classes.

Reconnect with Old pals: Reach out to old pals via social media or other channels. Reviving previous connections can be fruitful.

Supportive Services: Take into account registering with senior centers or using services geared for seniors. They frequently provide supplies and social activities.

Join travel clubs or groups if you appreciate exploring new places. It's a fantastic opportunity to meet new people and discover new locations.

Exercise Classes: Attend senior-specific fitness classes. It is beneficial to your health and gives you an opportunity to interact with others.

Encourage family get-togethers and reunions to keep your relationships with your loved ones intact. Attend networking events relating to your former field of employment or industry to maintain relationships with previous coworkers and develop new ones.

Seek Professional Assistance: If you're experiencing loneliness or despair, don't be afraid to contact a therapist or counselor for assistance.

Even though it takes work, creating a supporting network as a retiree can significantly improve your quality of life and offer the companionship and help you might need as you age.

☐ Mental Health in Retirement

Emotional well-being in retirement is a significant part of generally speaking prosperity. Retirement can bring huge life altering events, and what it means for your emotional well-being relies upon different elements, including your monetary security, social associations, and individual satisfaction.

Here are a few central issues to consider:

Planning your finances: Sufficient monetary making arrangements for retirement is critical. Monetary pressure can adversely influence psychological wellness. Ensure you have a financial plan and reserve funds plan set up.

Social Commitment: It is essential to Keep up with social associations. Keeping in touch with friends and family or joining a club or group can help alleviate feelings of loneliness and isolation.

Reason and Importance: Finding reason and purpose is vital for many in retirement. Think about seeking after leisure activities, chipping in, or investigating new interests to keep your brain locked in.

Actual Wellbeing: A solid way of life, including ordinary activity and a fair eating routine, can decidedly affect your emotional well-being.

Seek Help: Assuming you experience emotional wellness challenges in retirement, feel free to proficient assistance. Advisors or advocates can give direction and backing.

Design and Schedule: Keeping a day to day schedule can give strength and a feeling of motivation in retirement.

Recollect that everybody's retirement experience is novel, and it's fundamental to focus on your psychological prosperity during this period of life. A sign of strength and self-care is when you ask for help and direction when you need it.

Chapter 9

Navigating Legal and Regulatory Matters

☐ Scam and Fraud Protection

Be careful of spontaneous contact: Try not to answer startling calls, messages, or messages requesting individual or monetary data.

Confirm personality: Confirm the identity of the individual or organization contacting you before disclosing any information. Look into true contact subtleties freely.

Utilize solid, novel passwords: Secure your internet based accounts areas of strength for with, passwords and think about utilizing a secret phrase chief.

Be careful about speculation offers: Before making an investment, consult a reputable financial advisor and be wary of investment opportunities that appear too good to be true.

Screen bank and financial records: Check your financial statements on a regular basis for any unauthorized transactions.

Try not to give out delicate data: Never share your Government backed retirement number,

Federal medical care number, or banking subtleties except if you're sure it's genuine.

Shred confidential documents: Discard monetary records, like bank explanations, utilizing a cross-slice shredder to forestall fraud.

Remain informed: Stay aware of the most recent tricks and fakes focusing on retired folks through true sources and media sources.

Report dubious action: Report a scam or fraud to local authorities and relevant organizations like the Federal Trade Commission (FTC) if you suspect one.

Look for lawful guidance: Talk with a lawyer gaining practical experience in senior regulation to assist with safeguarding your freedoms and resources.

Keep in mind, tricksters frequently go after retired folks' trust and weakness, so consistently work-out alert and confirm data prior to making any move.

☐ Legal Documents Checklist

Here's a general checklist to consider:

Will

Establish a last will and testament to specify how assets should be distributed after death.

Living Will/Advance Healthcare Directive

Outline your healthcare preferences and appoint a healthcare proxy in case you cannot make medical decisions.

Durable Power of Attorney for Finances

Designate someone to manage financial matters if you become incapacitated.

HIPAA Authorization

Authorize specific individuals to access your medical information.

Financial Records

Organize financial documents such as bank statements, investment accounts, and retirement account details.

Insurance Policies

Review and update life insurance, health insurance, and long-term care insurance policies.

Beneficiary Designations

Ensure beneficiaries on retirement accounts, insurance policies, and bank accounts are up to date.

Property Documents

Maintain property deeds, mortgage documents, and any related paperwork.

Funeral/Memorial Instructions

Specify your preferences for funeral or memorial arrangements.

Social Security and Medicare Information

Keep these documents readily accessible.

Debt Information

Document any outstanding debts, loans, or credit card accounts.

Tax Returns

Store past tax returns and related records.

Trust Documents

If you have a trust, ensure it's current and aligned with your wishes.

Legal Contacts

Compile a list of important contacts, including your attorney, financial advisor, and healthcare providers.

Passwords and Online Accounts

Safeguard passwords for online accounts and provide access instructions to a trusted individual.

Identification

Maintain valid identification documents like passports, driver's licenses, and Social Security cards.

Safe Deposit Box

Keep a record of items stored in a safe deposit box, and provide access instructions.

Social Security and Pension Information

Gather documents related to your retirement benefits.

Long-Term Care Plan

If applicable, outline your preferences for long-term care arrangements.

Estate Planning Documents

Review and update any estate planning documents, including trusts and irrevocable life insurance trusts.

Remember that legal requirements and personal circumstances can vary, so it's advisable to consult with an attorney specializing in elder law to tailor this checklist to your specific needs and jurisdiction. Regularly update these documents as your situation evolves.

☐ Government   Assistance
Programs

There are several government assistance programs for retirees in many countries, but they can vary widely depending on your location. Common programs include:

Social Security (USA)

Provides a monthly income to retirees based on their work history.

Medicare (USA)

Offers healthcare coverage for individuals aged 65 and older.

Canada Pension Plan (CPP) and Old Age Security (OAS) (Canada)

Provides financial support to Canadian retirees.

State Pension (UK)

Offers a regular income to retirees based on their National Insurance contributions.

Age Pension (Australia)

Provides financial assistance to eligible retirees. Please specify your country for more detailed information or if you have specific questions about retirement benefits.

Chapter 10

Enjoying your retirement

☐ Achieving Fulfilment

Finding purpose, being active, and preserving social ties are all necessary for retirement fulfillment. To design a fulfilling retirement, think about hobbies, volunteering, or following lifetime passions.

☐ Creating a Legacy and Giving Back

As a retiree, leaving a legacy and giving back may be incredibly gratifying. Consider the following:

Mentoring: Helping out younger people in your community or profession is a great way to pass on your expertise and experience.

Spend time volunteering for issues or organizations that you are enthusiastic about.

Philanthropy: To support causes you care about, make donations to philanthropic organizations or establish a charitable foundation.

Family Values: Share your knowledge, customs, and morals with your loved ones and future generations. Write a memoir to inspire others by capturing your life's experiences and lessons.

Hold educational workshops or classes to impart knowledge of the abilities or pastimes you have acquired.

Participate in your community by joining organizations, boards, or committees to improve it.

Artistic Expression: Express your creativity through writing, music, or painting and make sure to show off your work.

Work with experts to guarantee that your assets and values are protected for the future through legacy planning.

Remember that creating a lasting legacy involves reflecting your values and interests in a way that positively impacts the world.

Conclusion

Finally, as you embark on this new chapter of your life, armed with the knowledge and techniques contained in this retirement plan book, keep in mind that retirement is a beginning, not an end. It's a time to celebrate newfound independence, pursue long-held ambitions, and savor precious times with loved ones. Your financial security and well-being are within your reach, and you may live a rewarding and worry-free retirement with careful planning and perseverance. May your retirement years be filled with joy, fulfillment, and the accomplishment of all of your retirement objectives. Congratulations on your well-earned retirement!